BLAZERS™

Disgusting Bugs

BY CONNIE COLWELL MILLER

Consultant:
Gary A. Dunn, M.S.
Director of Education
Young Entomologists' Society, Inc.
Minibeast Zooseum and Education Center
Lansing, Michigan

Capstone
press®
Mankato, Minnesota

Blazers Books are published by Capstone Press,
151 Good Counsel Drive, P.O. Box 669, Mankato, Minnesota 56002.
www.capstonepress.com

Library of Congress Cataloging-in-Publication Data
Miller, Connie Colwell, 1976–
    Disgusting bugs / by Connie Colwell Miller.
    p. cm.—(Blazers. That's disgusting!)
    Includes bibliographical references and index.
    ISBN-13: 978-0-7368-6798-6 (hardcover)
    ISBN-10: 0-7368-6798-8 (hardcover)
    ISBN-13: 978-0-7368-7876-0 (softcover pbk.)
    ISBN-10: 0-7368-7876-9 (softcover pbk.)
    1. Insects—Behavior—Juvenile literature. 2. Insect pests—Juvenile literature. I.
Title. II. Series.
QL467.2.M544 2007
595.715—dc22   2006026401

Summary: Describes 10 disgusting bugs and what makes them gross.

Editorial Credits
Mandy Robbins, editor; Thomas Emery, designer; Bob Lentz, illustrator;
   Jo Miller, photo researcher/photo editor

Photo Credits
Ardea/John Daniels, 9 (inset)
Dwight R. Kuhn, cover, 28–29
James P. Rowan Photography, 8–9, 10–11
Minden Pictures/ Mark Moffett, 17 (inset), 18–19; Stephen Dalton, 4–5
Nature Picture Library/John Downer, 12–13
NHPA/Anthony Bannister, 26 (inset); Mark Bowler, 26–27
Peter Arnold/ Becker & Bredel, 20–21; David Scharf, 14–15
Photo Researchers, Inc/Eye of Science, 6–7; Vaughan Fleming, 22–23,
     23 (inset); Volker Steger, 24–25, 24 (inset)
Visuals Unlimited/Dana Richter, 15 (inset); Larry Davenport, 19 (inset);
     Larry Kimball, 16–17

1 2 3 4 5 6 12 11 10 09 08 07

Table of Contents

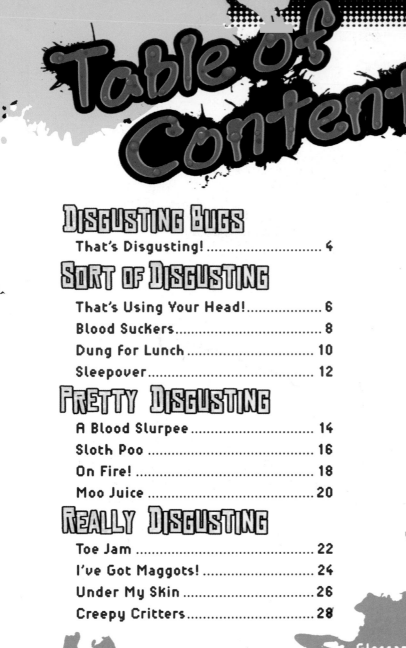

That's Disgusting!

Flies spit on their food. The spit helps soften the food so the fly can suck it up.

Creepy, crawly, buzzing, biting bugs can be pretty disgusting. They do gross things just to stay alive.

GROSS-O-METER

Use this meter to gauge how disgusting these bugs really are.

THAT'S DISGUSTING

That's Using Your Head!

Head lice are tiny bugs that can live on your head. They feed on blood and skin. Lice bites cause crusty, oozing sores.

GROSS-O-METER

SORT OF DISGUSTING

Blood Suckers

Ticks attach to humans and animals with their sharp mouthparts. Then they fill up on their victims' blood.

SORT OF DISGUSTING

GROSS-O-METER

A tick's body swells with blood after it eats.

A tick after eating

Dung for Lunch

Dung beetles love poop. They make balls of the stinky stuff and eat it. Some of them even burrow inside the balls and live there.

GROSS-O-METER

SORT OF DISGUSTING

Sleepover

Bedbugs can live in your bed. They poke holes in your skin and suck out blood while you sleep.

GROSS-O-METER

SORT OF DISGUSTING

A Blood Slurpee

When chiggers bite, their spit turns skin into liquid. Then chiggers crawl inside and slurp up the liquid like a milk shake.

GROSS-O-METER

PRETTY DISGUSTING

BLAZER FACT

Chiggers have spines that point backward. This makes it difficult to remove the bug once it is under your skin.

Chigger bites

Sloth Poo

Sloth moths live on animals called sloths. The moths lay eggs in sloth poop. When the eggs hatch, the young moths eat the poop.

GROSS-O-METER

PRETTY DISGUSTING

Sloth moth

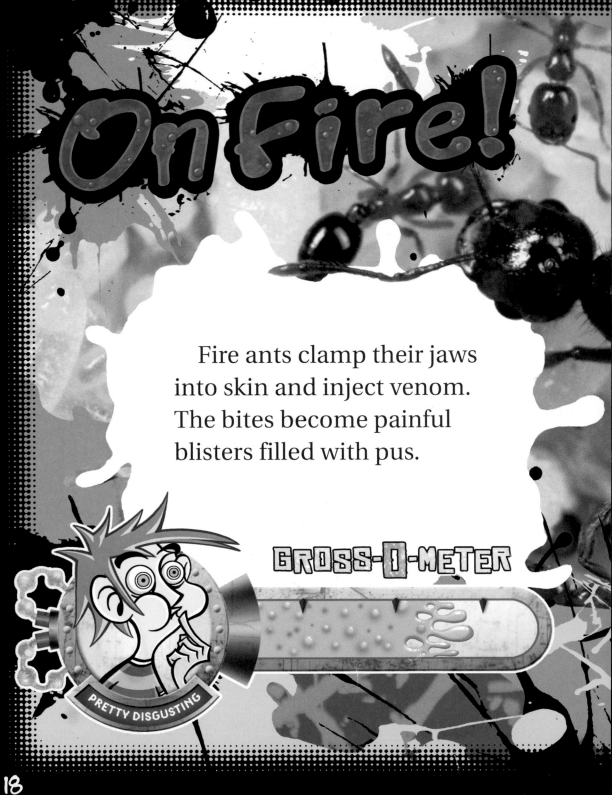

On Fire!

Fire ants clamp their jaws into skin and inject venom. The bites become painful blisters filled with pus.

GROSS-O-METER

PRETTY DISGUSTING

Fire ant bites

19

Moo Juice

Face flies suck up tears, snot, and drool from cattle and horses. Fly spit will keep an animal's eyes watering while the fly feeds.

GROSS-O-METER

REALLY DISGUSTING

BLAZER FACT

Almost 100 face flies can feed at the same time on the same animal!

Toe Jam

GROSS-O-METER

REALLY DISGUSTING

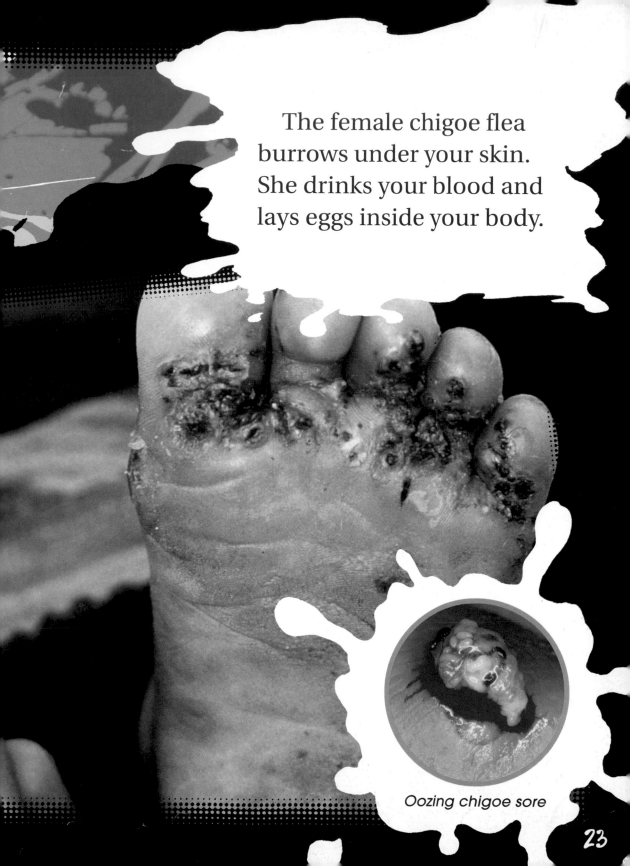

The female chigoe flea burrows under your skin. She drinks your blood and lays eggs inside your body.

Oozing chigoe sore

I've Got Maggots!

Cleaning the wound

House flies begin life as maggots. Maggots are often found on dead animals. Rotting bodies are their favorite meal.

GROSS-O-METER

REALLY DISGUSTING

Under My Skin

Adult bot fly

Bot flies glue their eggs to mosquitoes. When these mosquitoes bite you, they plant the eggs under your skin. The eggs grow until maggots pop out!

GROSS-O-METER

REALLY DISGUSTING

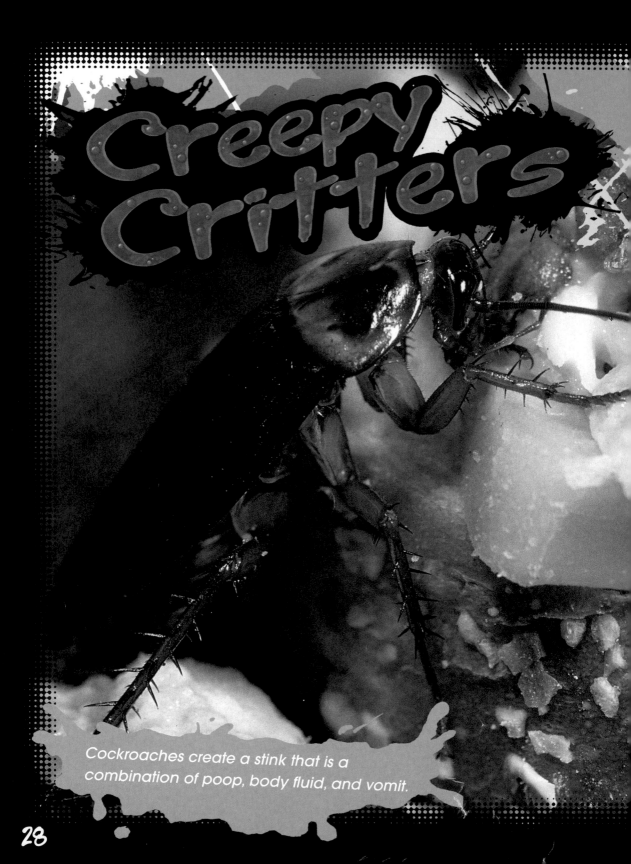

Creepy Critters

Cockroaches create a stink that is a combination of poop, body fluid, and vomit.

Bugs have good reasons for causing nasty sores, eating poop, and sucking blood. These disgusting behaviors help them survive.

We made it through, and I have one thing to say. **That's disgusting!**

Glossary

burrow (BUR-oh)—to dig a tunnel or hole

chigoe flea (CHIH-go FLEE)—a flea that buries itself in the skin of humans or animals and lays its eggs there

decay (dee-KAY)—to rot or break down

inject (in-JEKT)—to put into; some bugs and spiders inject venom into prey.

sloth (SLAWTH)—an animal with long arms and legs, curved claws, and a shaggy coat; sloths move very slowly and hang upside down in trees.

venom (VEN-uhm)—a poisonous liquid produced by some bugs and spiders

victim (VIK-tuhm)—a living creature who is hurt, killed, or made to suffer

Read More

Bathroom Readers' Institute. *Uncle John's Electrifying Bathroom Reader for Kids Only.* Ashland, Ore.: Portable Press, 2003.

Branzei, Sylvia. *Animal Grossology: the Science of Creatures Gross and Disgusting.* Reading, Mass.: Penguin Young Readers Group, 2004.

Szpirglas, Jeff. *Gross Universe: Your Guide to All Disgusting Things Under the Sun.* Toronto, Ont.: Maple Tree Press, 2004.

Internet Sites

FactHound offers a safe, fun way to find Internet sites related to this book. All of the sites on FactHound have been researched by our staff.

Here's how:

1. Visit *www.facthound.com*

2. Choose your grade level.

3. Type in this book ID **0736867988** for age-appropriate sites. You may also browse subjects by clicking on letters, or by clicking on pictures and words.

4. Click on the **Fetch It** button.

FactHound will fetch the best sites for you!

Index